OLD FIRST BAPTIST CHURCH.

HISTORY

OF THE

Newark Baptist City Mission

FROM ITS ORIGIN IN 1851

TO ITS

SEVENTEENTH ANNIVERSARY IN 1868.

BY

REV. EDGAR M. LEVY, D. D.

PUBLISHED WITH THE AUTHORITY OF THE BOARD.

NEW YORK:
PUBLISHED BY HURD AND HOUGHTON.
Cambridge: Riverside Press.
1869.

CONTENTS.

PART I.

PART II.

PART III.

PART IV.

PART V.

PART VI.

PART VII.

THE BAPTIST CITY MISSION

OF

NEWARK, NEW JERSEY.

Part First.

ORIGIN.

"A nameless man amid a crowd
That thronged the daily mart,
Let fall the words of hope and love,
Unstudied from the heart.
A whisper on the tumult thrown,
A transitory breath,—
It raised a brother from the dust,
It saved a soul from death.
O germ! O fount! O word of love!
O thought at random cast!
Ye were but *little* at the *first*,
But *mighty* at the *last*."

SOME of the most important and beneficent enterprises, both in the world and in the Church, have had their origin in what appeared an accidental, but what proved to be a providential, suggestion of the human mind. It was so in the origin of the Sunday-school work, by Robert Raikes; it was so in the origin of the British and Foreign Bible Society, and of the English Baptist Missionary Society. Results of infinite moment lie hidden in a passing thought, or in a simple suggestion. This fact is illustrated in the origin of the Newark Baptist City Mission.

Toward the close of the year 1851, the pastors of the First and South churches[1] were one day walking arm in arm, on Washington Street, when the former said to the latter, "I will tell you what I have been thinking about."

"And what is it, pray?"

"I have been thinking," said he, "that we ought to be planting some new churches in this growing city."

"It is a good thought," was the prompt reply; "it ought to be done."

Thus the conversation went on, till they

1 Rev. H. C. Fish, D. D., and Rev. William Hague, D. D.

were about to part, when it was agreed to speak to some of the leading brethren in each church, and get them together in the private parlor of Mr. John M. Davies, a member of the South Baptist Church.

Accordingly, on the evening of December 1st, of the above year, some ten or twelve persons met at the place designated, for consultation and prayer. At this meeting, the religious condition of the city, the demands of a constantly augmenting population, and the capabilities and duties of the Baptist denomination in Newark, were subjects of solemn and earnest consideration. The result was, that the following resolution was passed:—

"*Resolved:* That in the providence of God, there is a wide field for missionary labor in our city, and motives for its prosecution that should quicken us to renewed diligence and holy consecration."

It was also deemed desirable to employ immediately a missionary, and to open two places for preaching — one in the North Ward and another in the Fifth Ward, and liberal pledges were made for that purpose. A public meeting was arranged for, in order to secure the action of the whole denomination.

At this meeting, held in the First Church, December 7, 1851, an interest in behalf of the enterprise was manifested by the spontaneous contribution of additional sums, amounting to more than one thousand dollars. A plan of action was also adopted, by which each church was to elect six members, including its pastor, who should constitute a Board to direct the affairs of the Mission.

The first meeting of the delegates appointed to constitute this Board, was held on the evening of January 21st, 1852, in the lecture-room of the First Church. It was composed of the following persons: H. C. Fish, William Hague, David Jones, Lewis Nichols, John Compton, Samuel Mason, Sr., John Manning, Robert Johnston, John M. Davies, Daniel C. Whitman, Daniel M. Wilson. The Board was then formally organized by the election of proper officers.

Part Second.

PLAN OF OPERATIONS.

BEFORE proceeding to speak of the organization and support of churches, a few words of explanation may be necessary, in order that the constitution of the Board and the mode of operations may be clearly understood.

I. The Board has a legal existence. For some years its operations were prosecuted in a very limited and simple manner. But in the course of time mission property accumulated, and deeds of land for chapels and church edifices had to be secured. It was found necessary for the Board to be an incorporated body in order to hold property by law. The following act of incorporation was granted by the Legislature in 1861: —

STATE OF NEW JERSEY.

An Act to incorporate the Baptist City Mission.

1. *Be it enacted by the Senate and General Assembly of the State of New Jersey,* That Henry C. Fish, Daniel M. Wilson, Edgar M. Levy, Joseph O. Nichols, Robert Atkinson, Ebenezer Tingley, David T. Morrill, Joseph Morris, Charles W. Clarke, Daniel C. Whitman, and Conrad Bordenbender, and their successors, being members of the Baptist Church, be and they are hereby constituted a body corporate, by the name of the Baptist City Mission, and by that name shall have perpetual succession, and exercise and be clothed with the powers and privileges enumerated in the first section of the act entitled "An Act concerning Corporations," approved February fourteenth, eighteen hundred and forty-six, and shall be capable of holding, taking, and receiving by purchase, gift, grant, devise, bequest, or otherwise, and of conveying, mortgaging, and granting all such property and estate, real, personal, and mixed, which may be necessary or proper for the purposes and objects of the corporation, *provided*, that the yearly value of the property which said corporation shall at any one time hold or own shall not exceed Fifty Thousand Dollars.

2. *And be it enacted*, That the objects of said corporation shall be the furtherance and promotion of the interests of the Baptist denomination of Christians in the City of Newark, in this State, and its immediate vicinity.

3. *And be it enacted,* That the management of the affairs and concerns of said corporation shall be and is vested in eleven or more trustees, as the by-laws may direct, who shall be citizens of the said city of Newark, or its vicinity, and members of the said denomination of Christians (the persons named in the first section of this act to be the first trustees), a majority of whom shall constitute a quorum for the transaction of business; they shall be annually elected, and shall hold their first meeting at the call of said first trustees, and shall appoint a president, secretary, and such other officer and officers as they may deem necessary.

4. *And be it enacted,* That the trustees may provide by-laws to determine the number of said trustees to be annually elected; to provide for the election or appointment for their holding over in case the regular annual election should not take place and provide for filling vacancies, etc.

5. *And be it enacted,* That this act shall take effect immediately.

II. The members of the Board, or, according to the charter, the Trustees, consist of the pastor and four other members of each church, who are elected by the churches in April of each year.[1]

[1] Missions not organized into churches have the privilege of being represented by their missionary and one delegate, who may participate in the proceedings, but are not entitled to vote.

III. All the members of the Baptist churches of Newark are members of the City Mission. They are entitled to vote in their respective churches for those who are to represent them in the Board. They also have the privilege of organizing the anniversary meetings by the election of a Chairman and a Secretary; approving or otherwise the reports of the Board, and may give instructions to the same. They are likewise expected to contribute towards the object of the City Mission, *each one* doing *something*. Particular attention is given to interest *every member*, old and young, in this work of the extension of the Redeemer's kingdom.

IV. The Board meets on the last Monday evening of each month. The monthly meetings are conducted according to the following order: First, devotional services; second, calling the roll; [1] third, reading of minutes; fourth, treasurer's report; fifth, receipts of money from the collectors; sixth,

[1] Members not present at roll-call are fined twenty-five cents, unless detained by sickness or absence from the city.

reports of committees ; seventh, reports from the Missions; eighth, miscellaneous business; ninth, devotional exercises and adjournment.

V. At the first meeting of the new Board each year, one of the delegates from each church is appointed a collector for the church which he represents. It is his duty to keep a book and secure an annual contribution, if possible, from every member of said church. He reports to the Treasurer of the Board at each monthly meeting.

VI. The pastors and missionaries are expected to preach on the subject of city missions, and otherwise direct attention to the work of the Board, on the morning of the Anniversary Sabbath of each year. Subscription papers are then circulated through the congregation, to relieve, if possible, the collector from the labor of a personal application. Payments of subscriptions may be made to the collector, annually, quarterly, or monthly, at the pleasure of the subscriber.

VII. An annual and a semi-annual meeting of the City Mission are held. The annual meeting occurs on the second Sabbath in April, and the semi-annual on the second Sabbath in October.

These meetings, of late, have been held in the edifice of the First Baptist Church; the capacity of the house and its central location, making it all that could be desired for the gathering of the churches and the greeting of the Baptist Brotherhood.

At the annual meeting in April, it is the custom of the Sabbath-schools of all the churches and all the missions to proceed in a body to the First Church. The spacious galleries, and a part of the main body of the house, are usually filled with the children and their teachers, the remainder of the sanctuary being crowded with an attentive audience. It is impossible to give an adequate description of the beautiful sight presented at these annual meetings, or of the effect produced on the heart by all the children uniting to fill the house of the Lord with their songs of praise. Memorable, indeed, are those occasions, when the vigor of health, and the experience of age, and the flower of youth, and the fervor of piety, are found in beautiful combination, every one rejoicing in the success of the past and praying and planning for the work of the future.

VIII. The principal aim of the Mission is to encourage the organization of Sunday-schools, and to provide a preached gospel for the destitute in the growing sections of the city. The Board does not primarily propose to purchase lots and build meeting-houses. The usual course is to open schools and send forth missionaries, and leave the question of building chapels and the organization of churches to be developed by the success of the missions. The principle has been to follow, and not to precede, the guidance of Providence.

IX. It has also been a chief aim to preserve in the denomination in the city, "the unity of the Spirit in the bond of peace."

And this result has been happily realized. Like a generous, faithful, loving mother, the Mission has given to the new interests support, sympathy, and unwearied care. Like the eagle, she has borne them on her wings until they were able to go forth alone. Every month the missionary or pastor has come to the Board with a statement of the wants, the trials, the joys, or the sorrows of his particular charge. Here he has always found sympathy. Advice has been kindly given. Material aid has been generously voted, and sometimes special prayer has been offered that God would interpose, and do that which His own cause required, and which was beyond human power to accomplish.

The influence of these monthly meetings cannot be over-estimated. They have kept the channel of sympathy between the churches free from obstruction. They have checked the growth of selfishness, by opening fields of usefulness in which all have been called to work. They have cultivated unity and harmony among the churches, by affording opportunities of frequent intercourse with each other for Christian consultation and prayer. Here, in these monthly meetings, the members of the Board have grasped each other's hands, as messengers of the churches, in fraternal love. Here they have united in aggressive movements against the kingdom of darkness. Here they have proved to be " the helpers of each other's joys," and the bearers of each other's burdens in fulfillment of the law of Christ.

The moral power of such a union of the churches could not fail of producing the greatest possible amount of good. And its sweet spirit has often recalled the words of the Psalmist: " Behold, how good and how pleasant *it is* for brethren to dwell together in unity! *It is* like the precious ointment upon the head, that ran down upon the beard, *even* Aaron's beard: that went down to the skirts of his garments; as the dew of Hermon, *and as the dew* that descended upon the mountains of Zion: for there the Lord commanded the blessing, *even* life for evermore."

We may add, what lover of Zion has not had occasion to deplore the absence of such unity in our chief cities. Too often the constitution of churches results from unhappy divisions, or in some spirit that is not in accordance with that of the gospel. And too often the wealth and talent of the denomination has been concentrated and undeveloped in a single inert and overgrown body.

It is, perhaps, not too much to say, that could an unity like that realized in our city, be attained in other places, the strength of the denomination in those localities would be increased ten fold.

Part Third.

EARLY EFFORTS.

THE first act of the Board was to obtain a proper person to fill the position of missionary. Rev. C. W. Waterhouse was selected, who entered upon the duties of the mission in April, 1852. Regular services were established at 10½ A. M., in the third-story room of a store No. 102 Broad Street, and in Humanity Hall, in the Fifth Ward, at 3 P. M. Sabbath-schools were commenced at both stations. At first, the number who met on the Sabbath for religious instruction and worship was very small. As the Board, however, provided better accommodations, the attendance, both of the congregations and the Sabbath-schools, increased rapidly, while the missions grew in influence and usefulness.

Under the severe labors necessarily demanded by the cultivation of both these missions, situated in opposite parts of the city, the health of the missionary, Mr. Waterhouse, became so seriously impaired as to compel him to cease altogether from this service. On accepting his resignation, the Board caused the following to be recorded in the minutes:

"The Board would at this time bear testimony to brother Waterhouse's self-sacrificing labors, his fervent prayers, his consistent, devoted life in the cause of his Master, and his zeal for the Mission."

The work of this first missionary was that of the sower rather than of the reaper; but the seed planted under much discouragement has since borne fruit.

The Board called Rev. Thomas G. Wright to be his successor; and in April, 1853, he entered upon his missionary labors.

A chapel in the North Ward having been completed, mainly through the liberality of Messrs. D. M. Wilson and John M. Davies, the missionary was directed to give the chief part of his time to that field, the Board regarding it as the more promising. He preached, however, every Sunday afternoon in the Fifth Ward.

It was soon determined to employ another missionary. Accordingly, in October, 1853, David T. Morrill, a member of the Church at Rahway, and a graduate of the Rochester Theological Seminary, was invited to spend a Sunday in Newark. After preaching in the First and South Churches, he was elected by the Board as missionary for the Fifth Ward.

Mr. Morrill began his mission work the first Sabbath in November, 1853. The pulpit of the South Church becoming vacant by the resignation of Dr. Hague, Mr. Morrill, by the request of the Church and the consent of the Board, preached there for a time, on the Sabbath, and prosecuted his mission work during the week.

Under the faithful labors of the missionaries, the instructions of devoted teachers in the Sabbath-schools, and the prayerful and cheerful expenditure of the Lord's money, the cause of City Missions continued to bring forth fruit. Frequent revivals were enjoyed, and many, from time to time, were converted. These were added by baptism to the First and South churches. As these were the only two churches in the city at this time, there was no other way of gathering in those who were converted in the mission fields. The idea entertained by the Board at first was, to organize Sunday-schools, and hold prayer-meetings, and afford opportunities for hearing the gospel to those who lived in destitute parts of the city. It was not the intention to favor the constitution of churches until there was a sufficient number gathered in these missions to insure their permanency. Upon this theory, however, the missionaries worked under a great disadvantage. They were not able to retain in the mission as active workers those who had been converted. A wiser course was afterwards adopted. As soon as practicable churches were organized, and the converts were baptized by the missionaries, and became identified with the mission churches. This was found by experience to greatly facilitate the procuring of houses of worship, and the usefulness of the missionaries.

It will be seen by this that great care has always been taken by the Board in encouraging the organization of the churches. Not until the working force in any mission has given promise of success, and the Board, having counted the cost, has been prepared to furnish the necessary means so long as the church should require help, has an organization been favored. In this way, immature constitutions of churches, and those failures and disorganizations which have so often discouraged and grieved the denomination in other places, have been avoided.

The reproof which the Saviour administered to the man who commenced to build without counting the cost, is applicable to the organization of churches. It is wiser to wait years in laying the foundations securely, rather than to hazard a failure by an indiscreet and hasty movement. And yet too much caution, which may amount to timidity and weakness, must be avoided, lest the hearts of those who are laboring in the mission field should be discouraged by the impression that the cause will never rise to the dignity and responsibility of an independent church.

The Board has used great wisdom here; and so far no mission has been allowed to suffer from unnecessary delay, nor has any church, after its organization, been permitted to languish and expire for the want of support.

NORTH BAPTIST CHURCH.

Part Fourth.

ORGANIZATION OF CHURCHES.

THE NORTH BAPTIST CHURCH.

Constituted July 26, 1854.

HE mission in the North Ward, under the fostering care of the Board, and the labors of the missionary, Rev. T. G. Wright, had grown to such an extent within the two years of its existence, that the subject of organizing a church began to be seriously considered. At a meeting held in the chapel, June 11, 1854, Mr. H. M. Baldwin, of the South Church, moderator, the following resolution was adopted: —

"*Resolved,* That the time has come for the organization of a regular Baptist Church in the field now occupied by our mission station connected with the North Baptist Chapel in Orange Street."

This resolution was duly considered by the Board, and being approved, measures were immediately taken to organize a church. A council, composed of delegates from the churches of Piscataway, Orange, Plainfield, Bloomfield, Scotch Plains, Lyons Farms, Elizabeth, Jersey City, Hoboken, First and South Newark, met in the chapel, July 26, 1854. This council unanimously agreed to recognize the body as a regular Baptist Church under the name of the "North Baptist Church." The number of constituent members was forty-nine.

Public services of recognition were held the same evening, when Rev. O. S. Stearns, pastor of the South Church, preached the Sermon; Rev. H. C. Fish, pastor of the First Church, gave the Hand of Fellowship; and Rev. S. J. Drake, of Plainfield, the Charge.

Upon the succeeding Sabbath, July 30, the first member was admitted to the new church by baptism. In August, 1854, Rev. Mr. Wright, after performing much missionary labor, with fidelity and zeal, resigned his connection with the Board. The Church, with the advice of the Board, extended a unanimous call to the Rev. Levi Morse, to become their pastor. Nine hundred dollars were appropriated towards his support.

After a pastorate of nearly four years, during which time ninety-three were added to the Church, Mr. Morse resigned.

During the time of their destitution, the Church, through their delegates, were in frequent consultation with the Board, and prayer was more than once offered at the monthly meeting, that God would direct in the choice of a pastor.

May 10, 1858, the Church extended a call to Robert Atkinson, a licentiate of Fifth Church, Philadelphia. Mr. Atkinson accepted the call, and was ordained to the work of the Christian ministry, September 1, 1858, in the First Baptist Church. Soon after his settlement, the presence and power of the Holy Spirit became manifest in the meetings, and a season of extensive revival was enjoyed.

At a meeting held March 2, 1859, the Church resolved to enter at once upon the work of securing a more commodious house of worship. The little chapel, with which so many hallowed memories clustered, was no longer, either in capacity or convenience, suitable to the growing demands of the community in which it had been placed.

The Board was consulted. All the members felt the necessity of coöperating in the movement proposed. But at this time the denomination was engaged in assisting the First Church in building their large and expensive church edifice. This was the mother-church, and all were called to special effort and cheerful liberality. The strain upon the energies and resources of the Baptists of Newark was severe and long continued; but through the goodness of God the harmonious counsels and patient endurance of the brethren were crowned with success. The First Church was relieved of all financial embarrassment, and in the possession of a noble and attractive house of worship.

The way was now open to prosecute the building of an edifice for the North Church. A beautiful location, corner of Orange and High Streets, 140 by 70 feet, was selected and purchased for five thousand three hundred and fifty dollars.

In 1863 plans were adopted by both the Church and the Board, and a joint committee appointed to attend to the erection of the new chapel. In April, 1864, the Sunday-school room was occupied, and in the autumn of the same year, the remainder of the building was completed and dedicated to the service of God. The North Church paid towards this object the sum of two thousand five hundred dollars. By the sale of their old house and lot, four thousand more were realized. The First Church furnished fifteen hundred dollars; the South Church the same amount. In all, nine thousand five hundred dollars was raised in the city of Newark; and the remainder, about four thousand dollars, through the exertions of the pastor, was secured from abroad. This is the only instance in which help has been extended from sister churches out of the city.

Grateful mention should here be made of the Christian liberality of Mr. John M. Davies, whose name has already prominently appeared in these pages. Mr. Davies has removed from the city, but he still retains the warmest interest in the Mission which he helped to organize. For assistance in the erection of the chapel in the North Ward, and the new edifice which the church there now occupies, as well as the substantial aid rendered in the building of the two houses of worship which the South and First Churches occupy, the Baptists of Newark owe a lasting debt of gratitude to Mr. Davies.

Immediately following the dedication of the new chapel, a blessed work of the Spirit began, continuing for more than four months, resulting in greatly refreshing the Church, and adding to its number forty-four by baptism.

In 1865–66, thirty-three were added by baptism, and during the latter year only one month passed without witnessing the administration of the ordinance.

The Church commenced the year 1867 with a day of fasting and prayer, which was followed by a very quiet and gracious revival. Thirty-five were baptized. Unlike former seasons, the work began and continued among the adults, and quite a number of husbands for whom wives had long been praying, were brought into the fold.

In December of this year, the pastor, after a faithful and laborious ministry of ten years, resigned, in order to accept an appointment of the Board of the American Baptist Home Mission Society, for Kansas and adjoining States.

Not without years of earnest labor, accompanied by the cheerful sacrifice of time and means, and the earnest prayers and united efforts of the Church and the Board, have the results here sketched been attained. And who that looks at the attractive chapel of the North Church, occupying as it does one of the most beautiful sites in the city, and takes a survey of the field in which it has been planted, and contemplates the souls that have been gathered, can doubt that the labor and the money have been wisely expended?

It should here be added, that the benevolent contributions of this Church, since its constitution, have amounted to the sum of $3,950.22. The membership now consists of *three hundred and one.*

FIFTH BAPTIST CHURCH.
REV. D. T. MORRILL, PASTOR.

THE FIFTH BAPTIST CHURCH.

Constituted March 19, 1855.

THE mission in the Fifth Ward, as has been stated, was commenced simultaneously with that in the North Ward. After the division of the two fields, Rev. D. T. Morrill became the missionary for the Fifth Ward.

By request of the South Church, the Church at Rahway, of which Mr. Morrill was a member, invited a council to meet in the South Church, March 23, 1854, to consider the propriety of ordaining him to the work of the Christian ministry. The council met accordingly, and after an examination of Mr. Morrill, proceeded to ordain him by the usual services.

Mr. Morrill, being relieved in April, 1854, from his engagement with the South

Church, entered fully upon his work in the Fifth Ward Mission. During the ensuing winter, God was pleased to bless the preached Word, and quite a number of persons were converted. It then became apparent that a church organization was indispensable to the greatest efficiency and success of the Mission.

At a regular meeting of the Board, held March 5, 1855, after a full discussion, the following resolution was adopted: —

> "*Resolved*, that Rev. Mr. Morrill be instructed to obtain information as regards the material that can be gathered into a church organization, and report at a subsequent meeting."

At a subsequent meeting, held March 19, the missionary reported that fifty-six persons had voluntarily tendered their names as willing to become constituent members of a new church organization, and that these persons had subscribed four hundred and seventy dollars toward the support of the gospel for the first year; whereupon it was unanimously resolved, that in view of the circumstances, the Board recommend that a church be constituted at an early day in the Fifth Ward.

On Monday, March 26, 1855, a council convened in the South Church, in response to letters of invitation. The Articles of Faith and Covenant, adopted by the brethren, being satisfactory, the council recommended their recognition as a regular Baptist church, to be called the Fifth Baptist Church of Newark.[1] The public services of recognition were held on the evening of the same day. Of the fifty-six members constituting this Church, about an equal number came from the First and the South churches. The Church proceeded immediately to elect their missionary, who, by his faithful services, had endeared himself to them, to fill the office of pastor.

[1] This name has been objected to by many, as not being literally true. But considering the German Church as having precedence in point of time, the church is properly named. Another name would perhaps have been chosen ; but at the time of the organization, the church had no local habitation, and had been known as the Fifth Ward Mission.

The first Lord's day after the organization and recognition of this new Church, was one full of solemn interest and heavenly joy. Six new-born souls awaited the holy rite that should introduce them into Christ's visible Kingdom. The hearts of all were lifted in praise. After a brief morning service in the hall, the Church repaired to the South Church, where the ordinance of Baptism was administered. In the afternoon the Lord's Supper was celebrated for the first time by this infant body and these new disciples were welcomed by the hand of fellowship.

The great want of the Church now was a suitable place to meet in. It was evident to all that no very great and permanent growth could be expected with their present accommodations. In the early part of August the subject was earnestly discussed in church-meeting, and a resolution unanimously passed, that "immediate measures be taken for the erection of a suitable house of worship." A building committee was also appointed. In January, 1856, the building committee reported to the Church that Deacon H. M. Baldwin, of the South Church, who from the first had manifested great interest in this Mission enterprise, would give two lots on the corner of Lafayette and Prospect Streets, when a house costing not less than ten thousand dollars should have been built and paid for. Mr. Baldwin's proposition was thankfully accepted, and at the next meeting more than three thousand dollars were subscribed by those who were present, to be paid within two years, in eight equal installments.

The Church then, through its Trustees, presented the following memorial to the Board: —

"DEAR BRETHREN: — In the past we have been accustomed to look to you for advice and aid. This advice and aid, accompanied by the Divine blessing, has resulted in the formation of a church which God has so increased as imperatively to demand, in our opinion, the speedy erection of a commodious house of worship. A member of your Board, Mr. H. M. Baldwin, has magnanimously promised to deed to the

Trustees of this Church an eligible site costing two thousand two hundred and fifty dollars, when there shall have been erected and paid for, a house costing not less than ten thousand dollars. Pressed by the necessities of our present disadvantageous location, encouraged by this offer, and prompted by love to the cause of Christ, we resolved to make an effort within ourselves for the accomplishment of this object. And as the result of this, we have upwards of three thousand dollars subscribed. Thus situated we come to you for advice and aid. Shall the financial response be, 'Go forward?' when to go back is impossible, and to stand still imperils the cause? We desire a prompt and prayerful reply. If the remaining amount is subscribed by the other Baptists in this city, relying upon Divine aid, we promise to sustain ourselves thereafter.

"Yours, etc."

[Signed by the Trustees in behalf of the Church.]

To which the Board responded by pledging their hearty sympathy and coöperation. Plans for the church edifice were soon adopted by the building committee of the Church and the committee appointed by the Board.

The corner-stone was laid by the Rev. E. L. Magoon, D. D., September 15, 1856.

July 5, 1857, the lecture-room was dedicated with appropriate services. At once the congregation and Sunday-school began to increase. This was the year of the great financial convulsion, and the year also of the great awakening. In December, the Lord began to visit the church and congregation. The former was quickened to work and pray; the latter awakened to a sense of their sins and their need of a Saviour. The revival was of such power as to move through all the holiday festivities without hindrance. As the result of this visitation of the Holy Spirit, one hundred and twenty-three persons were baptized and received into the fellowship of the Church.

The house of worship having been finished and furnished, was dedicated to the worship of God, April 21, 1858. Dr. Dowling, Dr. Babcock, and Rev. A. Kingman Nott, preached on that day. A small debt remained on the new house. This debt, like many others of a similar nature, seemed difficult to pay. The finances of the country were disturbed, and the prospect was not encouraging. The Board was at this time paying four hundred dollars toward the support of the pastor. The Church had pledged the Board that it would ask no further aid as soon as their indebtedness was removed. It was seen that this amount was a large interest on fifteen hundred dollars, the sum yet owed.

Mr. James Hague, of the South Church, suggested to his pastor the following plan by which this debt could be removed, and the Church enabled to fulfill her pledge of self-support; namely, the Board to borrow the money, and get responsible persons to give *bona fide* notes with interest payable in two years.[1] Through the earnest efforts of Dr. Fish and Dr. Levy, the notes were procured; and though Mr. Hague died before the notes became due, and the amount borrowed was returned, yet the plan he devised secured the end.

[1] The money was borrowed from Dr. Rogers, of Paterson.

On the evening of January 3, 1860, Mr. Wilson, President of the Board, paid over the fifteen hundred dollars, thus removing all claims against the Church, while Mr. H. M. Baldwin, according to his pledge, gave them the deed of the lot on which the building had been erected. The Church unanimously passed a vote of thanks to these brethren, and then employed the remainder of the evening in prayer and thanksgiving to God for his gracious aid in the work of building a house for his glory.

The Church from this time has been self-sustaining — *giving* to the treasury of the Board instead of *receiving* from it. Through the blessing of God, and the generous co-operation of the City Mission Board, this result was reached in less than five years from the time the little band was organized.

The contributions of this Church since its organization, for benevolent objects, have amounted to the sum of $3,003.50. The membership now consists of *three hundred and ninety-seven.*

It will be also a matter of interest to state that during the past year, 1867–68, a very neat and commodious parsonage has been erected, adding greatly to the comfort and happiness of the pastor, a result which was much facilitated by the generosity of brethren who are members of sister churches.

In concluding this sketch we are moved to indorse the remark of the pastor, Rev. Mr. Morrill, that if the City Mission Board had done nothing more than to plant this *one* Church in all the years of its existence, it would have done a noble work. But this is only one, the second born, of the Mission Church sisterhood.

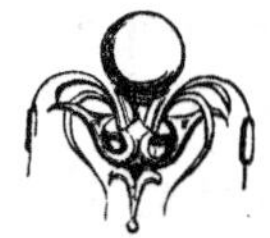

FAIRMOUNT BAPTIST CHURCH.

REV. W. D. SEIGFRIED, PASTOR.

FAIRMOUNT BAPTIST CHURCH.

Constituted June 29, 1860.

In the year 1859, the building, corner of Bank and Wickliff Streets, formerly used by another denomination, known as Fairmount Chapel, was reported to the Board as being unoccupied. Its location, the rapidly growing neighborhood, and the prospect of successfully establishing a mission there, were the subjects of thoughtful and prayerful consideration by the Board. The result was the opening of the place for worship, the organization of a Sunday-school, and finally the purchase of the property at a cost of over three thousand dollars.

For the first few months the pastors of the several Baptist churches preached alternately each Sabbath afternoon. The Sunday-school was under the efficient superintendency of Mr. D. C. Whitman, of the South Church, and grew rapidly in numbers and usefulness. In August, 1859, Rev. C. W. Clark was invited to preach in the chapel. This service resulted, soon after, in his call by the Board to assume the care of the Mission. On the 6th of October, Mr. Clark entered upon his labors. During the course of the winter the Mission enjoyed a quiet but refreshing revival. Twelve persons professed conversion, and the laborers in the vineyard were greatly encouraged.

January 19, 1860, the missionary was ordained to the work of the ministry, by a council called for that purpose by the South Church.

In April, thirty-eight persons signed a memorial to be presented to the Board, expressive of their views of the importance of a church organization, and seeking the advice of the Board. After mature deliberation, it was voted to approve of such a procedure. A council was called, and met in the chapel June 29. Twelve churches sent delegates. After religious services, a careful examination of the Articles of Faith, the prospects of the new Church, and remarks from several members of the Board, the council unanimously resolved to recognize the body as a regular Baptist Church under the name of the Fairmount Baptist Church. The services of recognition were held in the evening in the First Church. Rev. T. R. Howlett preached the sermon.

The new Church called to the pastorate Mr. Clark, who continued his relations with the Board, as their missionary.

During the course of that year, and especially in the winter of 1860–61, the Church received the most evident tokens of the Divine favor. The number of meetings was increased. The gospel became the power of God. Forty-eight were added by baptism, and twenty-five by letter.

In April, 1861, the Rebellion broke out, and the nation was called to arms. The sudden stoppage of almost all business so embarassed the Board, which had been appropriating to this Church six hundred dollars annually, as well as sustaining the other missions, that it was compelled to reduce the donation. By many it was feared that the pastor could not be sustained. But a system of personal weekly subscriptions was devised and immediately carried into effect. The pastor informed the Church that he would remain with them at all events and share their sacrifices. So wonderfully was the Church prospered under these scriptural efforts, that for the first time in its history it was enabled to pay the pastor's salary regularly upon the first day of each month.

The Board on several occasions assisted the Church in enlarging the chapel, and in otherwise adding to the comfort and efficiency of the congregation. But the Church felt an increasing necessity for better accommodations. Various plans were proposed, and as speedily abandoned, because the denomination had already all that it could sustain, — the North Church having just commenced its long delayed work upon its new house of worship.

May 30, 1864, the following resolution was adopted: —

"*Resolved*, That this Board recommend to the Fairmount Church to make an immediate effort towards the erection of a new house of worship."

A committee was also appointed to cooperate with a similar committee to be appointed by the Fairmount Church, to select and purchase a site for the proposed house. After a careful survey of the field, a location was finally selected on Bank Street, above Wickliffe, containing seventy-five feet front by one hundred feet deep. Measures were immediately taken to erect thereon a house of worship. Eight thousand dollars were at once subscribed by the several churches for that object. This amount was soon greatly increased, and the joint committees proceeded with the building. The corner-stone was laid September 12, 1866, by the Hon. T. B. Peddie, of the First Church, Mayor of the city; the address was made by Dr.

Dowling, of New York, and the various interesting services were participated in by the pastors of the several Baptist churches.

Sunday, May 19, 1867, the lecture-room was opened for public worship. Dr. H. C. Fish, Dr. E. M. Levy, and Rev. C. E. Wilson, Jr., preached on this memorable day.

In October of the same year, the pastor, Rev. C. W. Clark, who had so earnestly and faithfully labored for the interests of the Church, resigned the charge and accepted a call from the Church at Red Bank, N. J.

In July, the Church extended a call to Rev. W. D. Seigfried, who accepted the invitation, and entered upon his duties September 9, 1868. The edifice being entirely finished, was dedicated to the worship of God on the sixteenth of September. The contributions for benevolent objects since the organization of the Church, have been $931. The membership at the present time is *one hundred and sixty.*

MOUNT PLEASANT BAPTIST CHURCH.

REV. C. E. WILSON, JR., PASTOR.

MOUNT PLEASANT BAPTIST CHURCH.

Constituted November, 1867.

At a meeting of the Board, held November 27, 1865, an informal discussion was held on the prospects of the Eighth Ward as a field for missionary labor. This part of the city presented many attractions as a location. Broad Street — one of the finest avenues in the country — runs through it in a northerly direction. It is also on the direct road to Mount Pleasant Cemetery, the banks of the Passaic River, to Woodside and Belleville. The population was increasing, and improvements of the most substantial and attractive character were being constantly projected.

Other denominations had long been reported as designing to occupy the field, but as yet no signs of a movement were apparent.

Under these circumstances, the Board felt it to be their duty to make an effort to provide opportunities for religious worship for this destitute part of the city.

Mr. W. S. Hedenberg, the treasurer of the Board, had given much attention to the subject, but could find no place suitable for holding a Sabbath-school, or other religious services.

The Board listened with much interest to the statements made at this meeting by Mr. Hedenberg, and finally decided to appoint a committee, with power to purchase a lot on which to erect a mission chapel.

The committee reported January 29, 1866, that they had purchased a lot, seventy-three feet front on Broad Street, nearly opposite Governeur Street, and two hundred feet deep. Immediate measures were taken to build the chapel. In November, 1866, the chapel was finished and opened with appropriate services. The Sabbath-school was partially organized, November 19, 1866, and fully so December 3, 1866, by appointing Mr. D. C. Whitman, superintendent. There were in attendance at this time, fifty-four scholars and fourteen teachers.

It will be seen that the Board wisely purchased sufficient ground on which to erect an edifice such as this beautiful and growing portion of the city would, at a very early period, assuredly demand. The chapel might then be removed to the rear of the lot and used entirely for the Sunday-school and weekly services of a social character.

On the second Sabbath in February, 1867, Rev. C. E. Wilson, Jr., who had previously been pastor of the Baptist Church at Seaville, N. J., entered the field as missionary of the Board, preaching morning and evening. A formal welcome was extended to him on the afternoon of that day, in which the pastors of the various Baptist churches, with the pastor of the neighboring Methodist Church, participated.

The formation of the Church occurred in November, 1867, with thirty-one constituent members. Several conversions were soon after reported, and the Church and their faithful young pastor received early tokens of the Divine favor. Other denominations were provoked to zeal and good works; several chapels were soon erected in the immediate neighborhood, and thus the community was provided with the preaching of "the glorious gospel of the blessed God," and the children with instruction from loving and self-denying Sunday-school teachers.

THE PILGRIM BAPTIST CHURCH.

REV. SAMUEL BAXTER, MISSIONARY.

THE PILGRIM BAPTIST CHURCH.

Constituted, March 8, 1868.

IN the spring of 1860 a few members of the Fifth Church canvassed the Tenth Ward for the purpose of gathering into their Sunday-school the children who were destitute of religious education. These earnest Christians were much affected by the moral waste which they witnessed in this portion of the city. Their compassion for the neglected and the perishing, induced them to devise means for their recovery. They accordingly hired a small room in a private house, and opened a school in the afternoon of Sunday, May 27, 1860. At the first session there were present eight scholars. The school having been dismissed, the teachers remained for prayer. The hour for which the room was engaged having expired, they adjourned to the street, and there, under the shade of a tree, proceeded to elect their officers.

The school increasing in numbers, additional room in the same house was engaged. Other helpers, principally from the South Church, came in and offered their services.

At the monthly meeting in July, this new mission enterprise was reported to the Board. In accordance with the request of the Mission, it was voted that the Board approve the action of the brethren in establishing the school, and also of their collecting money to sustain it: and that it might be under the supervision of the Board, it was voted that the pastors of the South and Fifth churches, and one member from each of said churches, be a committee to counsel and superintend the Mission.

The school continued to increase in numbers and usefulness to such a degree, that its influence was apparent even in the personal cleanliness of the scholars, and the good order of the neighborhood. Sabbath-breaking and other forms of ungodliness were greatly diminished, and occasionally souls were converted.

The miserable accommodations, however, much impeded the working of the Mission, and limited the sphere of its usefulness. But with a zeal that could not be quenched, and a perseverance that must always command success, the Mission continued pressing its claims upon the denomination. At length Mr. H. M. Baldwin, of the South Church, purchased the house in which the school was held, and the adjoining grounds. Mr. Baldwin proceeded to give such a portion of this property to the Board as might be required to build thereon a chapel for the use of the Mission, besides subscribing liberally towards the building.

At a meeting held May 30, 1864, the Board recommended that all the churches make a collection the next Sabbath in behalf of this Mission. The churches, without exception, responded to this request, and liberal contributions were made on that day.

Necessary measures were at once taken to erect a neat and substantial chapel. A building committee was appointed by the Board, and the work was prosecuted with so much energy that the building was completed and opened for divine service early in July, 1864.

The following services were now held in the new chapel: preaching at 10½ A. M. by the German missionary, Sunday-school of the Tenth Ward Mission at 2½ P. M., and a prayer-meeting at 7½ P. M., besides several weekly meetings.

Mr. Samuel Baxter, having labored with acceptance and usefulness in the Mission in expounding the Scriptures, exhorting the people, and in visiting from house to house, was licensed by the South Church, of which he was a member, to preach.

In April, 1867, the Board appointed Mr. Baxter a missionary for the Tenth Ward, at the same time appropriating for the Mission five hundred dollars for the first year.

The subject of a church organization

was long and prayerfully considered by the Board, but for various reasons was deferred.

At the Board meeting in January, 1868, a committee was appointed to take the matter again into consideration. The committee met the teachers and others composing the Mission in the chapel on the evening of February 11, at which the subject was freely discussed. On motion a committee was appointed to report at a future meeting the names of such persons as would become the constituent members, should a church be organized. At a subsequent meeting, the committee reported thirty-six names, with a promise of others as soon as the organization should be complete. The committee of the Mission Board were requested to inform the said Board that it was the wish of the Tenth Ward Mission to become a regularly organized church.

The committee reported to the Board in accordance with this resolution, and the Board unanimously voted to approve of an organization of a church in the Tenth Ward.

On Sunday afternoon, March 8, 1868, a meeting was held in the chapel for the purpose of organizing a church. The committee appointed to apply for letters of dismission, reported that there had been received twenty-eight letters from the South Church, five from the Fifth Church, and two from Fairmount Church. The persons bearing these letters proceeded to organize themselves into a church. Measures were also taken to call a council of recognition. At a subsequent meeting the name of "Pilgrim Baptist Church" was unanimously adopted.

The council met, and after examination unanimously voted to proceed to recognize the body as a regular Baptist Church. The public services were held in the evening; Rev. H. F. Smith, of Bloomfield, preached; Rev. D. T. Morrill gave the Hand of Fellowship, and Dr. Levy delivered the Charge.

FIRST GERMAN BAPTIST CHURCH.

REV. JULIUS C. HASSELHUHN, PASTOR.

Part Fifth.

GERMAN CHURCH AND MISSION.

THE FIRST GERMAN BAPTIST CHURCH.

Constituted September 7, 1849.

REV. K. A. Fleischman, whose mental and moral worth, and earnest labors in behalf of his "kinsmen according to the flesh," have secured for him so large a place in the hearts of American Baptists, has the honor of being the first German Baptist minister in this country. He arrived in New York in March, 1839. Receiving an invitation to preach in Newark, he came to stay one Sabbath, but was induced to remain. Many of the Germans, however, finding that he would not sprinkle and confirm their children, but would preach only those doctrines and administer only those ordinances for which he could find authority in the Scriptures, became bitterly opposed to him. But the Lord was with him, blessed his labors, and permitted him, in October, 1849, to baptize three persons, the first Germans in this country who received the ordinance from a German Baptist minister.

Mr. Fleischman soon after this time left Newark to labor in Pennsylvania. He continued, however, to make frequent visits to this city, and from time to time souls were converted under the preaching of a pure gospel, and added to the little band of baptized believers. They united with American Baptist churches, but continued to hold among themselves regular meetings in German.

After long and patient waiting, their heart's desire was fulfilled by the organization of a German Baptist Church, September 7, 1849.

The Church was recognized September 20, 1849, by a council consisting of delegates from the following churches: South

Baptist Church, New York; First German Baptist Church, New York; and First Baptist Church, Newark. The council was organized by appointing Dr. Summers, of New York, moderator. Immediately after the recognition services, the council proceeded, by request of the Church, to examine the pastor elect, with the view of ordaining him to the gospel ministry. The examination being satisfactory, Mr. S. Küpper was solemnly ordained by prayer and the laying on of hands. Mr. Küpper having resigned his charge March 1, 1850, the Church were without a pastor more than eighteen months.

In October, 1851, Mr. A. Hüni was ordained to the work of the ministry in the First Baptist Church, by the request of the German Church which had called him to be their pastor. The number of their membership had increased to thirty.

After a successful pastorate of four years, Mr. Hüni resigned February 7, 1856, the Church having then fifty-eight members.

A call was extended to Mr. Conrad Bordenbender in August, 1856. Mr. B. was ordained in the First Baptist Church, August 26, 1856. Mr. Bordenbender labored earnestly for over five years, during which time the membership increased to ninety. He resigned October 31, 1861.

The Church called Rev. J. C. Haselhuhn, of Wilmington, Del., who began his labors in Newark, January, 1862. Until 1861, the Church suffered greatly for the want of a house of worship, having always met in hired rooms, sometimes unfavorably located and otherwise inconvenient. The necessity of a proper place for worship was keenly felt by their American brethren as well as by themselves. The subject was more than once introduced and discussed at the anniversary meetings of the City Mission.

In February, 1859, the Church resolved to make an effort to secure a house of worship. Committees were appointed; one to solicit subscriptions, and the other to select a proper place. Subscriptions among themselves soon amounted to over a thousand dollars. The Church then resolved to lay their case before the City Mission Board. The Board kindly received them and gave them much encouragement. It was also voted that the German Church be invited to appoint delegates to represent them in the Board. A committee consisting of D. M. Wilson, of the First Church, J. O. Nichols, J. M. Barrows, and R. Johnston, of the South Church, was appointed to coöperate with the German Church in selecting a location for a house of worship. About this time the German Presbyterian Church in Mercer Street, above High Street, was offered for sale. The joint committees were unanimously in favor of purchasing the same. The Church, February 5, 1861, authorized the Mission Board to buy it for them, at the price of twenty-five hundred dollars, which was accordingly done. Thirteen hundred dollars, which the German brethren had raised among themselves, was paid on it. The balance the Board became security for, besides repairing and putting the house in good order.

The dedication services were held April 7, 1861. In the morning the dedication sermon was preached by Rev. K. A. Fleischman, of Philadelphia. In the afternoon a general meeting was held, and addresses made by Drs. Fish and Levy. In the evening interesting services were held in German, and the occasion was one of joy and gladness to the little band who had been so long without a religious home.

In 1864 an effort was made to pay off the debt that still remained against their chapel. The Church raised two thousand, and the balance was paid by the American churches. These results placed the German Baptists in Newark in a position for aggressive movements among their countrymen.

The contributions of this Church for benevolent objects have amounted to $4,092.93. The number of members is *two hundred and twelve.*

TWELFTH WARD MISSION CHAPEL.
REV. J. C. KRAFT, MISSIONARY.

THE TWELFTH WARD MISSION.

THE increase of the German population has been a marked feature in the growth of the city. In every direction they have been building homes for themselves, and extending their influence. The Twelfth Ward was so largely composed of this element as to attract the attention of the members of the German Baptist Church. The delegates from this Church brought the condition of the Ward before the Mission Board. The Board at once appointed a committee with instructions to secure a place suitable for a Sunday-school. No better place could be found than a private house which had been a drinking-saloon. This was rented and opened as a mission station. The second Sunday in June, 1863, a Sunday-school was organized with one hundred scholars and sixteen teachers. Religious services were held immediately after school, and the pastor of the German Church, Rev. J. C. Haselhuhn, preached regularly every Sunday afternoon for more than one year.

As the field needed more labor than Mr. Haselhuhn could bestow upon it, a missionary was appointed at a salary of six hundred dollars, who began his labors in September, 1864, but resigned in a few weeks after his appointment. Rev. A. Transchel entered upon the work soon after, and preached acceptably to the Germans in both the Tenth and Twelfth Wards, until his removal to Buffalo, in 1866.

In May of the same year, Rev. C. Kraft, of New Brunswick, was appointed at a salary of eight hundred dollars.

As the dwelling-house in Niagara Street proved entirely inadequate for the Sunday-school and mission, a committee was appointed by the Board to select suitable lots and erect a chapel. A location corner of Niagara and Patterson Streets was purchased, and a commodious chapel was erected thereon, at a cost of about five thousand dollars. The dedication of this new house of worship occurred on Sunday afternoon, September 4, 1866.

The field has thus far proved to be an exceedingly hard one. Romanism and infidelity are predominant. The missionary can only reach them by much self-denial, and by visiting from house to house. A few, however, have been converted, and the Sunday-school contains at present over one hundred and fifty children. Through the power of the gospel which is being preached by a faithful missionary, and the earnest labors of the members of the German Baptist Church, there is much to encourage the friends of Christ, that a time of ingathering will come, and in place of the little chapel will be erected a substantial and attractive church edifice. The Germans are attracted by good and commodious houses of worship, and are exceedingly fond of music. While it is not proper to encourage extravagance in either, yet it is wise to consult the taste and education of men in all things that are lawful. Fidelity to our own principles does not necessarily involve a blind and bigoted opposition to everything that differs from our habits and customs. Things indifferent should be allowed to be indifferent, and all our zeal and fidelity concentrated on what is essential both in faith and practice.

FIRST BAPTIST CHURCH.

REV. HENRY C. FISH, D. D., PASTOR.

Part Sixth.

SKETCHES OF FIRST AND SOUTH CHURCHES.

FIRST BAPTIST CHURCH.

Constituted June 6, 1801.

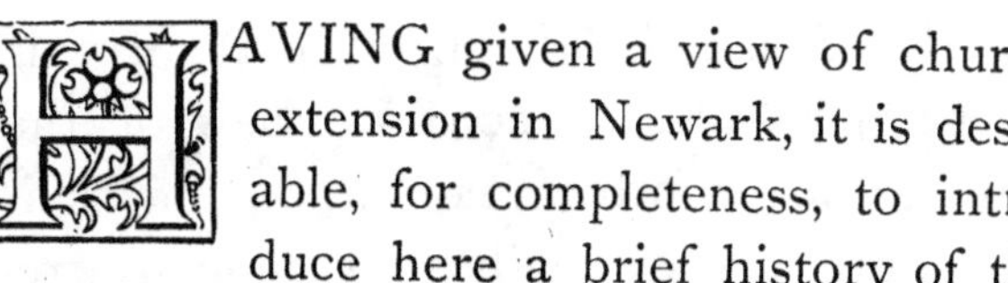

HAVING given a view of church extension in Newark, it is desirable, for completeness, to introduce here a brief history of the two churches out of which this movement sprang.

The First Church was formed on the 6th of June 1801, of five brethren and four sisters, all except two members of the Lyons Farms Baptist Church, one of the oldest in the State. Worshipping at first in a schoolhouse, and struggling forward in great weakness, it was not until the year 1806 that they were able to occupy a home of their own, which consisted of a small meeting house, 35 by 45 feet, on Academy Street, corner of Halsey Street. This church edifice was taken down and replaced with one 48 by 68 feet, and costing over $5,000, in the year 1810. And yet again, in 1841, this house underwent thorough repairs and improvements, consisting, in part, of the addition of a vestibule and lecture-room, at a cost of $3,000. The picture of the old First Church edifice, in the front part of this volume, presents an accurate view of the house in its improved condition, and as it stood until it was finally sold upon the removal to a new location.

Of pastors, the Church has had fourteen. The progress of the cause, in its outward manifestation, can best be seen in the two tables which are here given.

The following table presents, at a glance, the Pastors, their term of service, the number of Members at the commencement of each one's ministry, the number he baptized, and the time of closing his ministry: —

Names of Pastors.	Commenced Labors.	With Members.	Number Baptized.	Closed Labors.	Years.	With Members.	Gain.	Loss.
Rev. Charles Lahatt . . .	February, 1802	17	16	July, 1806 . .	4+	32	15	–
Rev. Peter Thurston . . .	March, 1808 .	35	29	March, 1809 .	1	54	19	–
Rev. Daniel Sharp, D. D. .	April, 1809 .	53	6	November, 1811	2+	71	18	–
Rev. John Lamb	April, 1812 .	62	3	April, 1813 .	1	59	–	3
Rev. David Jones	January, 1814	72	80	November, 1821	7+	112	40	–
Rev. Daniel Putman . . .	April, 1822 .	109	8	May, 1824 . .	2—	108	–	1
Rev. Ebenezer Loomis . .	December, 1826	108	9	June, 1827 . .	1—	107	–	1
Rev. C. F. Frey	January, 1828	109	5	April, 1830 .	2+	111	2	–
Rev. P. L Platt	April, 1830 .	111	10	April, 1831 .	1	113	2	–
Rev. Daniel Dodge	August, 1832 .	120	94	February, 1839	7—	213	93	–
Rev. William Sym, D. D. .	April, 1839 .	213	86	May, 1843 . .	4	261	48	–
Rev. Henry. V. Jones, . .	September, 1843	259	96	April, 1850 .	7—	368	109	–
Rev. E. E. Cummings, D. D.	July, 1850 . .	339	–	November, 1850	1—	339	–	–
Rev. Henry C. Fish, D. D. .	January, 1851	330	920*	† †	18†	863*	533*	–

* Up to 1868, inclusive,
† Term of service not expired.

The following table exhibits the Number of Baptisms, and the Number of Members, for any given year up to the present time, December, 1868: —

Year . .	1801	1802	1803	1804	1805	1806	1807	1808	1809	1810	1811
Baptized	—	6	2	4	2	2	11	13	16	23	4
Members	13	17	33	36	34	33	34	46	60	88	84
Year . .	1812	1813	1814	1815	1816	1817	1818	1819	1820	1821	1822
Baptized	2	1	6	2	2	37	28	3	0	2	3
Members	64	?	70	72	82	110	122	120	120	112	109
Year . .	1823	1824	1825	1826	1827	1828	1829	1830	1831	1832	1833
Baptized	4	1	1	9	7	2	1	2	8	8	14
Members	112	108	102	102	103	107	110	111	113	120	128
Year . .	1834	1835	1836	1837	1838	1839	1840	1841	1842	1843	1844
Baptized	9	12	23	12	9	7	48	13	11	7	6
Members	149	164	203	221	216	213	257	264	270	261	306
Year . .	1845	1846	1847	1848	1849	1850	1851	1852	1853	1854	1855
Baptized	7	7	30	9	7	30	42	25	21	106	36
Members	322	331	372	380	376	339	378	391	433	550	492
Year . .	1856	1857	1858	1859	1860	1861	1862	1863	1864	1865	1866
Baptized	25	18	236	19	29	25	11	6	125	16	152
Members	462	495	730	703	716	709	697	673	777	751	901
Year . .	1867	1868									
Baptized	13	15									
Members	900	863									

From the foregoing tables it will be seen that the Church has been destitute of pastoral care for more than nine years. Also, that in the remaining forty-one years, up to the present pastorate, the average term of service was about two years and eleven months. The most protracted pastoral service, except the present, was rendered by David Jones; the second in length, by H. V. Jones; the third, by Daniel Dodge; and the fourth, by Charles Lahatt and William Sym. Deducting the time of service of these five brethren, the average length of the pastorate under the nine remaining ministers, was but about one year and four months. The present unfinished pastorate extends thus far through eighteen years.

The total number of additions to the Church by baptism up to the present pastorate, was 511; since then, 919; total since organization of the Church (sixty-seven years), 1430. Average per year for the first fifty years, a fraction above 10. Average per year since then, a fraction above 51.

The periods of the greatest weakness and severest trials of the Church, have been those of its most frequent change in the pastoral relation.

The darkest period in the history of this Church was in the winter of 1811 and 1812. The flock was without a shepherd, scattered, distracted by internal dissensions, and threatened with pecuniary calamity. The following action as to a Church debt tells its own story:—

> "*Moved*, That brethren James Beach and Jabez Pool be a committee to wait upon Mr. ———, informing him of the impoverished state and truly distressing circumstances of the Church. *Resolved*, To throw ourselves entirely on the clemency of Mr. ———, trusting alone in the mercy of God to direct the affair, and in submission to His will, wait the event."

But, although this Church, particularly in its early experiences, had many and sore trials, its history as a whole is luminous with the goodness of God. And it must be noted, that its *missionary* era was the era of increasing strength. When it began to care for others, God especially cared for it. In 1836, twelve members disconnected themselves from the parent body, and formed the Second Baptist Church in Market Street, under the supervision of Rev. P. L. Platt. But in less than five years the Society disbanded; and it appears that the movement was ill advised. With this exception, the First Church stood as the sole American Baptist body in Newark until the expiration of a half century, when the South Baptist Church was constituted, as the result of a true Christian enterprise.

The benevolent contributions of the Church cannot be fully ascertained. There is extant a memorandum bearing the date of 1818, showing that that year $11.00 were given to the New York Missionary Association. In 1834 it was reported to the New York Association that the Newark Church had given $167.00 to benevolent objects. In 1836 the sum was $675.00; in 1846, $1,108.00; in 1847, $1,192.57; and in 1848, $1,558.54.

The following table presents at a glance the aggregate yearly benevolent contributions of the Church so far back as statistics can be obtained: —

1849 $1,861.04	1850 $1,204.36	1851 $1,566.08	1852 $2,034.00	1853 $3,242.34
1854 $3,872.00	1855 $2,242.25	1856 $2,855.00	1857 $4,395.00	1858 $2,275.00
1859 $1,090.50	1860 $2,092.44	1861 $1,525.00	1862 $1,025.00	1863 $550.21
1864 $2,351.00	1865 $3,815.00	1866 $6,900.00	1867 $14,350.00	1868 $12,600.00

The total of these figures for twenty years is $64,946.22; or an average of $3,247.31 a year.

Besides these sums given for missionary objects, the pecuniary strength of the Church has lately been severely taxed in the erection of the new church edifice; the corner-stone of which was laid October 4, 1858, and which was dedicated May 23, 1860. The necessity of a new house had long been felt; and the undertaking was only deferred that the City Mission work, sketched elsewhere, might have the benefit of the united energies of the denomination. But the accessions to the membership from the "Great Revival," and other circumstances, intensified the demand for more ample accommodations.

The first formal movement in this direction was at a Church meeting held April 23, 1858, when the subject of a new house was introduced and favorably considered, but laid over to a special meeting. The following is a copy from the Church Records of the doings of the meeting held by appointment: —

"A special meeting, April 26, 1858, of the Church and congregation was convened by a call of the Trustees publicly read from the pulpit. Opened with singing and prayer. After which D. M. Wilson was called to the chair, and Isaiah Peckham was appointed Secretary. The Chairman stated that the object of the meeting was to take into consideration the propriety and necessity of erecting a new house of worship for the accommodation of the Church. Brother Andrews requested that the first chapter of Haggai might be read. The pastor read the chapter. After an informal exchange of views, brother Andrews offered a resolution: 'That the time has come in the providence of

God when we are imperatively called upon to proceed in the erection of a new house of worship.' The resolution was unanimously adopted, and the vote was very large. Subscriptions were then taken up amounting to the sum of $10,800."

Building and finance committees were appointed, and in June the plan of the house was voted upon and adopted; the carpenter work being assigned to the skillful and faithful hands of one of the members, Deacon David D. Dunn.

It was intended from the first that there should be no Church debt upon the house when completed; and the supposition was, that the subscriptions actually obtained, or easily available, would cover the expense, the old house and lot paying for the new lot. But the financial panic of 1857 and 1858, and the breaking out of the civil war, disappointed these expectations. The subscriptions in great part could not be collected, and the old Church property did not find a ready sale, so that the interest on the purchase-money of the new lot had to be annually paid, besides providing for the

Church debt proper. The generosity of the congregation was again and again brought into requisition, and some almost wearied of giving, and despaired of ever seeing the end of pressing dues and persistent appeals. The financial ability of an efficient Board of Trustees, and the utmost help of pastor and people, scarcely sufficed to meet the emergency. Indeed, about the beginning of 1863, an unpaid claim was so far pressed that the Church property was technically in the sheriff's hands. This perplexed and embarrassed state of mind on the part of the brethren from pecuniary troubles, seriously impaired the spiritual condition of the Church; but no one could discover a door of deliverance. At his own instigation, Dr. Fish visited Mr. John M. Davies and a few other liberal brethren in New York city, and laying before them the whole case, obtained a subscription of several thousands of dollars, *conditioned* upon the payment of the whole debt of $25,000, except that upon the Church lot (which was soon afterward met by the disposition of the old property). This subscription from a neighboring city agreeably surprised and gave heart to the members of the Church and congregation, and it was determined to make one effort more to sweep away the encumbrance. The strain was heavy alike upon the pastor and the brethren and the Baptists generally in the city; but through the mercy of God the attempt was crowned with success, and sincere thanksgivings upon the following Sabbaths ascended to heaven from a worshipping assembly, at length free from debt.

The following, taken from a copy of the "Examiner," bearing date February 26, 1863, may here be fittingly introduced:—

"The First Baptist Church in Newark, N. J., of which Dr. H. C. Fish is the pastor, has done itself honor. They had hoped to enter their new house of worship free from debt. But this hope was frustrated by the financial troubles of the times, and the Church has, for some time, been burdened by an unpaid balance of $25,000. The members of the Church were moved by a holy ambition to attempt to shake off the incubus, and by their generous efforts, and with the help of a few friends in New York, they have now provided for every dollar of the debt. The Church is much rejoiced at its freedom. We heartily congratulate not only our Newark friends on the energy and generosity with which they have ensured success for their enterprise, but also Baptists in general on the evidence which this movement gives of the prosperity of one of the largest of our churches."

The edifice thus completed and paid for, is located in the centre of the city, upon Academy Street, and within a few rods of the largest avenue, Broad Street. In its main parts it is built of brown chiseled stone, in the Romanesque style of architecture, extending one hundred and seven feet in depth, by seventy-two feet front; and is surmounted by two turrets, each one hundred and twelve feet high. The first floor is divided into a Lecture Room, forty-two by sixty-six feet, two Social Rooms, or Church Parlors, twenty-five by thirty-three feet (which three rooms may be converted into one by sliding partitions), and an Infant Class and Library Room. The second floor, or main Audience Room, is intersected by four aisles, with permanent sittings for about fourteen hundred persons. The Singers' Gallery and Organ are behind the pulpit, at a slight elevation, to facilitate congregational singing. The Baptistery is immediately under the pulpit, the floor of which is its movable cover, and has Retiring Rooms on either side. The whole building is every way substantial, attractive, and convenient, and cost, with the lot and the furnishing, about $50,000, which is not one third of the present value of the property.

Revivals of religion have been a marked characteristic of this Church. Particular mention should be made of seasons of awakening in the ministries of brethren Sym and Jones, and those of more recent years. The most remarkable of these gracious visitations was that which is denominated the "Great Revival," in 1857 and 1858. As this period was memorable all over the land for God's converting power, and perhaps in no place more so than in Newark, the nature and results of the powerful work in the First Church may here be properly put upon permanent record.

The earliest indication of a better state of things, was an intense yearning for its existence. This was seen, particularly, in the latter part of December, by which time the Sabbath preaching and week-day evening remarks looked almost wholly to a holier and more earnest and active state of the Church. As yet, however, this deep solicitude was limited to a very few individuals,— apparently not more than half a dozen besides the pastor, and at the first, not even to so many. Where it did exist, it was almost crushing; and particularly on one occasion, at an evening prayer-meeting, the burden of spirit was so great on the part of the pastor, as to incapacitate him for the conduct of the meeting, and he sat in his chair giving way to suppressed sighs and tears, leaving the meeting to take care of itself.

About this time one extra weekly prayer-meeting was held, and after a little, two; and finally, perhaps threescore of the brethren and sisters met every evening, by common consent, to pour out their prayers to God, and to talk of the languishing state of Zion. No souls had as yet been converted, if indeed awakened; and it was often remarked, that it was not desired that the brethren should sing and pray and talk too much about the conversion of sinners; they were not yet thoroughly reconverted *themselves;* and it was needful that the work "*get roots*" in their own hearts, by confession and supplication and exhortation, and the alternations of hope and fear. The tree would be the more fruitful by cropping and pruning it severely. When the Church was right — at least a *small part* of it — *then* it would be time to turn attention to sinners.

Not long, however, was it possible to restrain the rising desire for the salvation of others. The longing was towards dying men; and it is remembered that one brother wished (to use his own expression) that the Lord would give them *one* kid over which to make merry. The boon was not long withheld. *One* soul of the few unconverted in the meetings, was awakened and renewed, and then another; others came, and others still; the meetings increased, and soon were transferred, *of necessity*, from the lecture-room to the body of the house. These meetings were continued nearly every evening till near the middle of May.

When the work was reaching its greatest strength, and the audience-room was crowded, even to the extra seats, it was suggested by some whether another minister might not be invited to labor with the pastor, and so economize his strength, and save him, perhaps, from entire prostration. It was concluded, however, with one mind, to call in no outside help, but to look to the Lord, and pray and labor on. With the exception of a single week, when the pastor was called away to visit a sick mother, resort was not had to outside help. Indeed, this has not been done in any of the revivals.

The specific form of effort was the *prayer-*

meeting. Not a solitary *sermon*, as such, was preached, except on Sunday, and then only two. Even the usual weekly lecture was dispensed with. But the exposition and enforcement of the *inspired word* were never more constantly brought into requisition. After the opening of the meeting, ten or fifteen or twenty minutes were always given to this exercise. The design was, especially, to open up, and affirm and re-affirm, in every possible way, the two great facts of theology — man a sinner, and Christ a Saviour — and to press home the duty of an *immediate* attention to the things of salvation. Christ was continually insisted upon and held up to view as the Saviour of the lost, and the Word of God was never more honored of God as the chosen instrument unto salvation. Almost every Sabbath-discourse, particularly, seemed to fall with power upon the congregation eager to receive it; and the fruits were perceptible during the week, in the awakening or relief of souls.

Besides pastoral visitations, an *inquiry*

meeting was held an hour before the ordinary evening meeting, in the lecture-room, where each one present was conversed with personally, and the way of salvation was minutely explained and illustrated. This means was greatly blessed. Two *tracts* should be mentioned as especially useful: "Don't Put it Off," and "What is it to believe on Christ." Hundreds of the latter were given away, and in scores of instances did God employ this silent messenger to bring light and relief. In later works of grace, the forty-eight page tract, "Two Questions,"—"Is your Soul Safe?" and "How can I be Saved?" were greatly useful. It should alsobe said, that the brethren and sisters, especially the Sabbath-school teachers and converts, were active in exhortation and invitation, and God owned and blessed abundantly their labors.

There was not much speaking in the prayer-meetings, except in some stages, by the *converts*, nor much singing; *praying* was the main feature. Every exercise was *short* and *spirited.* Not unfrequently *special* prayer was offered at the close of the meeting, for those who were so oppressed with feeling as to be unable or unwilling to leave. At these seasons, six or eight of the brethren, out of the few that tarried, oftentimes prayed. When the work looked like ceasing, prayer-clusters of this kind were formed to pray to God for its continuance; and cases of awakening were always multiplied. The anxious were never invited forward, but such as desired prayers were requested, towards the close of the meeting, to arise. This act of committal was often attended with great good.

The number of conversions it is impossible to ascertain; probably it would reach three hundred, at least. Two hundred and thirty-five were baptized, most of them recent converts. Of these, one half were heads of families — fathers and mothers. About one hundred of the two hundred and thirty-five were males. A larger number were over forty than under twenty years of age; the average being about thirty. About two thirds of those added, were unaccustomed before to worship with this Church, either attending nowhere, or holding connection with other congregations. As far as possible they were all put at work in the Sunday-school and elsewhere. The younger portion organized themselves into a Young Converts' Prayer-meeting, and the older into an Adult Converts' Prayer-meeting.

As another result, the gifts of the previous members were materially developed and improved, and new attainments were made in the divine life. It is believed that the moral power of the Church was doubled in the space of a few months.

Some of the main features of this remarkable work were the following: —

1. *The evident presence of the Holy Spirit.* It was of God, and not of man. The Spirit went before, the preacher and laborer followed after.

2. *Clearness and depth of conviction for sin.* Moralists suddenly saw themselves

to be the chief of sinners, and stout and hard-hearted men were made to weep like children under a sense of their guilt and danger. In several cases, awakened men were unable to prosecute their daily business, and not unfrequently did the anxious tell of their sleepless nights, and their deep burden of spirit. In one case, a man sitting up to pray until after midnight, seemed, as he said, to be sinking through the floor; and rising from his knees, could scarcely walk. In another, a sturdy man, hitherto unmoved, was seen standing in the vestibule of the church, with his long beard all jeweled with the tear-drops that were rolling from his eyes. Another man declared that he had carried a "cannon ball" in his heart for days together, and that if it had been continued for three days longer he could not have lived. He could neither sleep nor eat; and yet, a few days before, he was as unmoved as a rock. In another case, a man in middle life came to see the pastor, and on entering the house, cried aloud as he told of his sins, and was so agitated that he trembled from head to foot, and could scarcely sit in his chair. Several times, while he was being told what he must do to be saved, he burst out crying, and exclaimed, "*O, but I have been such a sinner!*" Another man wholly suspended his work, stayed at home, read his Bible and prayed, and seemed to be actually waxing poor in flesh from intense concern of mind. He was the picture of despair. All these were men in mature life, and hitherto self-righteous moralists.

3. *A clear insight into the way of salvation through Christ, on the part of the converts.* In most cases, the sum of the answer for the hope of salvation, was, "*Christ died!*" In most cases, it was *the sight of the cross* that brought relief. As a consequence, the converts were generally *strong*, and went on their way obeying and rejoicing. Taken as a whole, the relation of experiences was satisfactory in the highest degree.

4. *Its freedom from noise and excitement.* No careless observer would have perceived anything remarkable. The meetings were uniformly solemn, almost like a funeral: — no audible groanings or rejoicings, and nothing whatever to which the most fastidious could take exception.

5. *The honor put upon prayer, and the ordinary means of grace.* Answer to prayer was oftentimes direct and almost instantaneous. In some of the most earnest and importunate of combined supplications, the brethren were as conscious that they were heard above, as if it had been expressly revealed to them. *Directness* in prayer was a marked feature. Now, *the one point* was the awakening of sinners; now, the relief of the burdened; and then again, the efficiency of the word preached. Beyond these three things the range of prayer did not often extend, and in some cases, the wrestling rose well-nigh to an agony of spirit. Lay-agency was greatly honored, and, as already remarked, the plain and pointed preaching

of the gospel. Such, in some of its main features, was one of the most precious awakenings with which a Church was ever blessed.

Large numbers of the converts gathered during revivals, and at other seasons, have in late years been dismissed to help in the formation of new churches within the limits of the city. This has also been true in respect to the experienced members. To give up these beloved brothers and sisters, often the tried helpers of the pastor, has been a real sacrifice. In the nature of the case, it must have called into exercise enlargedness of view and unselfishness of feeling. But it is believed that wherever one has felt it to be duty to go out and strengthen the weak places in Zion, no obstacle has been laid in the way; while, on the other hand, the whole spirit of the preaching has tended in the direction of earnest individual exertion. Certainly those dismissed from this body within less than twenty years would make several efficient churches.

But, with a present harmonious membership of more than eight hundred and fifty souls, and perhaps the largest Sabbath audiences of any denomination in the State; with a Sunday-school averaging nearly five hundred; with an average charitable distribution each year of more than ten thousand dollars, besides a generous outlay for current expenses; and with the exercise of its full proportion of moral power in the community where it is planted, the First Baptist Church of Newark may be instanced as an example of the divine principle, that "there is that scattereth and yet increaseth:"—a point which is prominently dwelt upon in the closing chapter of this work.

SOUTH BAPTIST CHURCH.

REV. EDGAR M. LEVY, D. D., PASTOR.

HISTORY OF THE SOUTH BAPTIST CHURCH.

Constituted February 13, 1850.

IT is conceded by all, that the erection of the South Church gave the first impulse to the spirit of city missions. For nearly fifty years the Baptist cause had been in a dormant state. A small frame building on Academy Street accommodated all who could be induced to attend public worship conducted by Baptists. But little money was raised, and but few efforts were made for the enlargement of Zion. The limits of the city had extended on every hand, the population had increased at a wonderfully rapid rate, and other denominations had grown from three to seven fold, and yet during all this time the Baptists had appeared satisfied with their ill-constructed meeting-house, and with the limited influence they were exerting in the community. The gospel had been preached among them by able and faithful ministers, but there were few comparatively who seemed moved by it to a reception of Christ, while the piety of many of these even, was of a sickly and feeble type, like the health of children who have been long confined, and have had no opportunity for physical exercise or for breathing the pure air of heaven.

It pleased God at last, however, to move the hearts of a few worthy men to break up this spell of self-satisfaction. At several meetings of the Church, and on the street and elsewhere, the subject of church extension and Christian enterprise was introduced and earnestly advocated. These brethren, feeling deeply the necessity of expansion, and moved with holy zeal for the advancement of Christ's kingdom, finally succeeded in awakening an interest in behalf of the movement in the minds of others.

At a meeting of the Church in 1849, a

committee was appointed " in order to take measures for the erection of a new church edifice, and for the organization and permanent establishment of a new Baptist interest in addition to the one now existing."

In accordance with this resolution, a lot on the corner of Broad and Fulton streets was soon after purchased. Failing, however, to obtain a satisfactory title, the property was abandoned, and the attention of the committee was directed to the southern part of the city. A location, Kinney Street near Broad, was at length selected, and measures were immediately taken to erect a neat and substantial structure for the worship and glory of God.

At a meeting held in the lecture-room of the First Church, February 13, 1850, of persons holding letters of dismission for the purpose of forming a new Church to occupy the edifice then in course of erection, Mr. Edward Doughty was chosen Moderator, and M: D. C. Whitman, Clerk. After prayer, the Moderator requested persons holding letters of dismission, for the purpose for which this meeting was called, to present them. The following was read: —

"At a regular meeting of the First Baptist Church in the city of Newark, N. J., held February 13, 1850, the following brethren and sisters, members in regular standing with us, were, at their own request, dismissed to form a new Baptist Church to worship in the house now being erected by this Church, in Kinney Street in this city, namely: Edward Doughty, John M. Davies, Alice S. H. Davies, Louisa Davies, Robert Johnston, Ann L. Johnston, Samuel Baldwin, Mary Baldwin, Mary Belcher, David Jones, Mary Jones, Jane B. Hedden, Emma Ely, James Hague, Anna Hague, Daniel C. Whitman, Abraham Runyon Jr., Sarah Ann Runyon, Jane Morris, Rebecca Shuart, Caleb H. Earl, Elizabeth H. Earl, Mary M. Earl, Mary Canfield, George P. Morrow, E. P. Morrow, Catherine Fowler, George H. Bruen, Mary Bruen, George M. Foster, Mary Law, Lydia Ann Force, Julia Wilson, Maria Hedden, Isaac Scribner, Caroline Scribner, I. Camfield. May the blessing of God attend the formation of this new interest, and the same unanimity and Christian harmony ever characterize the intercourse of the two sister churches which prevail between us and these dear brethren and sisters.

"By order and on behalf of the Church.

"ISAIAH PECKHAM, *Church Clerk.*"

The persons named in this letter, who were present, were requested to arise and thereby signify their assent to the formation of this new Church. Prayer was then offered by Mr. David Jones. Articles of Faith were adopted, and a covenant read and approved. South Baptist Church, Kinney Street, Newark, New Jersey, was adopted as the name by which this Church should be known. Mr. George H. Bruen was elected clerk.

At a subsequent meeting the following additional names were presented, and by vote were received as constituent members: Ebenezer T. Kirkpatrick, Joseph O. Nichols, Eliza D. Nichols, Abraham Coles, John H. Cross, Nancy Johnston, Mary Earl, John Rees, — in all forty-five members.

With great unanimity the Rev. William Hague, D. D., of Boston, was called to the pastorate of the Church. On motion, a council of delegates from Baptist churches was called to meet in the First Church, on the first Tuesday in March, for the purpose of publicly recognizing the body as a regular Baptist Church. This council convened according to the request, Tuesday, March 5, 1850, when, after an examination of the Articles of Faith, and the manner of their organization, it was unanimously resolved to proceed to recognize them as an independent church of Christ. The services were held the same evening in the following order: reading of the Scriptures and Prayer by the Rev. H. C. Fish, of Somerville, N. J.; Sermon by the Rev. E. L. Magoon, D. D., New York, from Psalm cxix. 18; Right Hand of Fellowship by Rev. H. V. Jones, pastor of the First Baptist Church, Newark, N. J.; Charge to the Church by Rev. S. J. Drake, Plainfield, N. J.

The Lecture-room of the church edifice was opened for worship, April 14, 1850. Dr. Hague, the pastor, was present for the first time, and preached in the morning from Mark iv. 34. "Vestry services" was the subject of the discourse. In the afternoon, the twenty-first chapter of John was expounded, and the small meetings of the disciples, with their beloved Master as their teacher, was the subject.

July 18, 1850, the church edifice being finished, was opened for public worship. Dr. Hague preached from Ephesians iv. 21.

This enterprise, so auspiciously begun, sent a thrill of vital energy through the whole body. It was now seen what might be accomplished by the united efforts of the Church of Christ in devising liberal things.

The South Church continued to prosper under the able discourses and faithful labors of its distinguished pastor. Our principles, as a denomination, were so clearly defined, and so scripturally maintained, that many from other denominations were convinced and became obedient to the truth. Many also, among the unconverted, were awakened by the Spirit of God, sought mercy through Christ, "believed, were baptized, and added to the Church."

The Church likewise abounded in generosity. Liberal donations were made from time to time, towards the extension of Christ's kingdom in the city and throughout the world. Very early in the history of the Church, the subject of systematic benevolence claimed special attention. In July, 1850, Dr. Hague made the following report: —

"NEWARK, *July* 2, 1851.

"The Committee appointed to consider and propose a plan for regular and permanent contribution to objects of benevolence, report, —

"That they regard the object before them as one of the most important that can now engage the attention of the Church. As with us it is an acknowledged truth that a church is Christ's appointed instrumentality for the extension of His kingdom on the earth, the question which relates to a plan of contribution is one which bears directly on the grand design for which the Church was constituted. To the Corinthian Church the Apostle said, 'Therefore as ye abound in everything, in faith, in utterance, in knowledge, in all diligence, and in your love to us, see that ye abound in this grace also,' that is, liberal giving. Hence it is evident that God has made it the duty of a church to promote His cause, not only by contending earnestly for the faith once delivered to the saints, but also by the contribution of property.

" In writing to this same Church, to whom the words just quoted were addressed, Paul gave the following direction : 'Upon the first day of the week let every one of you lay by him in store as God has prospered him, that there be no gatherings when I come.' At that time a special object of benevolence was before the Church of Corinth, and the Apostle wished all the members of it to contribute systematically and from principle, with quietness and efficiency, so that he might not appear among them as a fiscal agent seeking for money. The direction which we have cited involves several important principles.

" First, that Christian benevolence should be conducted according to a system. It should not be left to the mere play of impulse or the excitement of circumstances.

" Second, that this system should be comprehensive and pervasive. 'Let every one lay by him.' Let the sick and the poor meet together with their offerings of love at the altar of Christ.

" Third, that the designation should be made at a stated time, frequently as often as once a week. On the first day of the week, when we thank God for redemption and salvation, then we are bidden to lay a tax on our worldly income or expenditure, and to place it as a tribute of gratitude at the Saviour's feet.

" Fourth, this weekly study and calculation of the amount of our contribution should lead us to give to an extent commensurate with our power of giving. 'Let every one lay by as God has prospered him.'

"Here we have developed the apostolical plan of benevolence; a system of God's ordering — simple, equal, rational, effectual; requiring nothing to sustain it in any church but that degree of love to Christ and His cause which will keep us from forgetting Him longer than the interval between successive Sabbaths. If we have real love to Him, that system would be found to be self-sustaining, and we have reason to believe that the result would prove that the hints of Scripture are better than volumes of man's wisdoms.

"In view of these considerations, which might be more largely urged, the Committee recommend, —

"First, that a collection be taken after the sermon, on the morning of every Sabbath, for the cause of evangelization.

"Second, that from the funds thus accruing to the treasury of the Church, appropriations be made to specific objects of benevolence, at such times as may be hereafter designated.

"All which is respectfully submitted.

"Wm. Hague."

This was the beginning of a system of Sabbath offerings which has secured a large amount of money in the aggregate, and has been a continual source of blessing to the Church. This system of benevolence was farther modified in 1865, when Dr. Levy, by direction of the Church, presented the following plan, by which the contributors know, at all times, the objects which are claiming their offerings and their prayers:

"The custom, recommended by the Apostle Paul, and established by this Church at its organization, is still cherished by us as eminently the wisest and most successful and becoming arrangement for securing the contributions of God's people. It is but right that every Christian, as he comes to the sanctuary 'on the first day of the week' to worship God and to give thanks 'for His unspeakable gift,' should bring with him a portion of the fruits with which God has crowned his labors. The rich should give of their abundance, the poor of their frugal savings, and all should give cheerfully and according to the measure of their ability.

"The collections on each Sunday morning will be appropriated to the following objects and in the order now designated: —

"January and February, Foreign Missions; March, American Baptist Publication Society; April, Newark Baptist City Mission; May, Sunday-schools; June, American Baptist Home Mission Society; July and August, Miscellaneous Objects; September, American and Foreign Bible Society; October and November,

New Jersey Baptist State Convention; December, New Jersey Baptist Education Society, and the Ministers' and Widows' Fund."

November 2, 1853, the Church was called to bear their first trial. Dr. Hague, their esteemed pastor, after a pastorate of about three and a half years, resigned his charge.

The Church was supplied with preaching by Rev. D. T. Morrill, until March 12, 1854, when a call was extended to Rev. O. S. Stearns, of Southbridge, Mass. Mr. S. entered upon his duties May 7, 1854, on which occasion public services of welcome were held, in which several ministers of the city and vicinity participated.

This second pastorate, which was so satisfactory to the Church, was destined to be of short duration.

December 17, 1854, by permission of the Church, Rev. Dr. Sears presented himself as a messenger from the Baptist Church at Newton Centre, Mass., and described the need of the Church there, and made an urgent appeal that the South Church would relinquish their claims upon their pastor, and consent to his accepting the call which had been made by the Church he represented.

The South Church, through a committee, addressed a letter to the Church at Newton Centre, declining to comply with their request. The pastor, yielding to the warm expressions of affection and of earnest wishes that he would not sunder the ties which bound them together, publicly announced, January 14, 1855, that he would remain with them.

Efforts, however, continued to be made by the Church at Newton Centre, to induce Mr. Stearns to accept their invitation. These efforts at last succeeded. August 29, 1855, after a pastorate of about fifteen months, Mr. Stearns resigned his charge.

Rev. J. L. Hodge, D. D., was called to the pastoral charge of the Church, October 3, 1855. He accepted the invitation, and in November entered upon his labors.

During the pastorate of Dr. Hodge, many

were converted, and a large number of persons, who from indifference had lost their membership in other places, having been induced to renew their vows, were received by the Church on experience. Dr. Hodge resigned November 8, 1857, after serving the Church just two years.

Rev. J. H. Walden supplied the Church for three months.

In June, 1858, the present pastor, on his way to fulfill an engagement with an esteemed brother in the ministry in a neighboring city, was induced to stop at Newark and supply the pulpit of the South Church one Sabbath. He preached from Col. i. 19. "That in all things He might have the preeminence." God gave him such favor in the eyes of the people that, although he left the city early the next morning, measures were immediately taken to have him return and preach for them again. In July, he complied with their request. This second visit resulted in the Church extending to him a call to become their pastor.

It was not for some time after that the call was accepted. The relationship which bound him to his people in Philadelphia had been of fourteen years existence. It was his first and only pastorate. Nearly the entire membership had been baptized by him, and only a high sense of duty and the prospect of greater usefulness, could prevail on him to accept the call to the Church at Newark.

On the first of October, 1858, he entered upon his duties here. The Church and congregation had become much discouraged and weakened by the frequent changes in the pastoral office. But soon the blessing of God attended the ministrations of his servant, and frequent additions by baptism, and an increase of attendance on the means of grace imparted hope and encouragement to all.

In 1859 a large and elegant organ was introduced, by the aid of which, with the change in the hymn book, the service of song in the house of the Lord was much improved.

In 1860 there were constant tokens of the Divine favor, and conversions were reported every month. In the midst of this success, however, the pastor was suddenly prostrated by an alarming illness, which laid him aside for nearly three months. In answer to the earnest and loving prayers of the Church, the Lord was pleased to permit him to resume his labors among them.

In 1862 the exterior of the church edifice was repaired and greatly improved. The front was faced with brown stone, which gave to it a substantial and neat appearance.

In 1863, through the efforts of the pastor and the liberality of the Church and congregation, the interior of the sanctuary was remodeled and beautified. The plans and the execution of the work are highly creditable to the architect, Mr. David S. Gendell, of Philadelphia, and to the decorator, Mr. John Gibson.

During the winter and spring of 1864 the Church enjoyed a precious "season of refreshing from the presence of the Lord."

Sixty-eight were baptized and received into fellowship.

Again, in 1866, the Lord poured out His Holy Spirit and the Church was greatly revived. Nearly one hundred souls were baptized, and the membership reached almost five hundred, being the largest, except one, of any Baptist Church in New Jersey.

In 1868, the Pilgrim Baptist Church, in the Tenth Ward, was organized. This Church grew from the mission planted there eight years ago, by members of the Fifth Church. The principal support, however, has always been derived from the South Church. The ground on which the chapel stands, as well as most of the cost of erecting the same, were liberally donated by Mr. H. M. Baldwin, of the South Church, "whose praise is in all the churches;" while nearly the entire constituent membership went forth from this Church, with its blessings and its prayers accompanying them.

According to the statistics of the Church,

the total number of additions has been as follows: Number of constituent members, *forty-five*. During the pastorate of Dr. Hague, from April, 1851, to November, 1853, three years and a half, by baptism, *ninety-one;* by letter, *one hundred and fourteen;* by experience, *three;* total number, *two hundred and eight.*

During the vacancy in the pastoral office, from November, 1853, to May, 1854, by baptism, *twelve;* by letter, *two;* total number, *fourteen.*

During the pastorate of Dr. Stearns, from May, 1854, to August, 1855, fifteen months, by baptism, *twenty-five;* by letter, *thirty-eight;* by experience, *one;* total number, *sixty-four.*

During the pastorate of Dr. Hodge, from November, 1855, to November, 1857, two years, by baptism, *forty-eight;* by letter, *fifty;* by experience, *sixteen;* total number, *one hundred and fourteen.*

During the vacancy, from November, 1857, to October, 1858, by baptism, *fifteen;*

by letter, *fourteen;* total number, *twenty-nine.*

During the ten years of Dr. Levy's pastorate, by baptism, *two hundred and fifty-two;* by letter, *one hundred and seventy-three;* by experience, *thirteen;* total number, *four hundred and thirty-eight.*

The entire number received from all sources since the Church was formed, is *nine hundred and twenty-four. Three hundred and forty-seven persons* have been dismissed by letter, *forty-six* have been excluded from the fellowship of the Church. and *sixty-four* have "fallen asleep."

The first named, we may charitably hope, are now useful and consistent members of sister churches; the second, the excluded, awaken many painful thoughts and excite the prayer that they may, through the abundant mercy of God, be restored to repentance and good works. The last, those who have fallen asleep, lead us to say, "Blessed are the dead which die in the Lord!" How precious is the memory of Samuel Baldwin,

Ann L. Johnston, James Hague, Edwin R. Parsil, Edward Doughty, David Jones, Mary Jones, Mary Baldwin, and many others of whom "we cannot now speak particularly."

"With us their names shall live
Through long succeeding years,
Embalmed with all our hearts can give, —
Our praises and our tears."

Part Seventh.

GROWTH FROM EFFORT.

A PERIOD of seventeen years has thus elapsed since the Newark Baptist City Mission Board was organized. In conlusion, let us survey the field and sum up the work.

As before stated, in December, 1851, several members of the First and South churches met for consultation and resolved to organize for the prosecution of City Mission work.

In April, 1852, the first missionary employed by the Board entered upon his duties. Two places for worship and for Sabbath-school instruction were opened, one in the North and the other in the Fifth Ward.

In 1853 the first chapel, erected for the Mission, was dedicated to religious worship in the North Ward.

In the same year a reinforcement to the working force of the Mission was made by the appointment of another missionary, who was assigned to the Fifth Ward.

July 26, 1854, the North Ward Mission was organized into a Church, with a membership of forty-nine, composed mostly of such persons as had been converted through the instrumentality of the Mission.

In 1855 the Mission in the Fifth Ward was organized into a Church with fifty-six constituent members.

April 21, 1858, the new edifice of the Fifth Church was dedicated.

In May, 1859, the Fairmount chapel was purchased by the Board, and opened for worship; the pastors, in their turn, preaching every Sabbath afternoon. A Sunday-school was also established. October 6, the Board engaged Rev. C. W. Clark to labor here as a missionary.

January 3, 1860, the debt on the Fifth Church was paid through the efforts of the Board, and the Church henceforth became a self-supporting body.

June 29, 1860, the Fairmount Mission was organized into a regular Baptist Church.

February 5, 1861, a house of worship was purchased for the use of the German Baptist Church, the members of which exhibited great liberality and Christian zeal in the accomplishment of this long desired object.

July, 1864, the chapel in the Tenth Ward was completed, paid for, and opened for the use of the Mission. A German missionary was also engaged, who preached there in the morning, and in the afternoon at Hamburg Place, where a German mission had been established.

About this time the Board also engaged the services of a German colporteur.

November, 1866, the Mount Pleasant Mission was organized. A neat chapel was opened for religious services.

February, 1867, Rev. C. E. Wilson, Jr., was engaged by the Board, and entered upon his work in the Mount Pleasant field.

May 19, 1867, the lecture-room of the Fairmount Baptist Church was dedicated.

During this year (1867) a missionary was engaged by the Board for the Tenth Ward Mission.

March 8, 1868, the Pilgrim Baptist Church was constituted in the Tenth Ward.

Thus in seventeen years the Board have planted six missions, employed nine missionaries and one colporteur. They have aided in the organization of five churches, assisted in the building of three substantial houses of worship, and four chapels. Through the advice and liberality of the same, the Germans have secured their house of worship, besides a commodious chapel, and have the services of an efficient missionary.

Through the direct influence of these missions, and the faithful labors of the missionaries, *one thousand and fifty-four persons* have been baptized and added to the churches. There has been expended for the support of the missions *twenty-nine thousand four hundred and eight dollars*, besides the large outlay in building church edifices proper for the Fifth, the North, and Fairmount churches, and much of the cost of the *chapels* for other posts, which has not been included in the above estimate, and of which no account has been preserved.

Without the moral and material assistance thus afforded by the Board, some of these churches would never have been established ; or if they had, their existence would, in all probability, have been feeble and of brief duration. Without this, the church edifices and chapels which now dot the different sections of the city, diffusing light and love, joy and gladness throughout the community, would never have been erected, and the missionaries, who have been preaching the gospel, and laboring for the salvation of souls, would not have been sustained. Those thousands of dollars, so productive of good and great results, could not otherwise have been raised, concentrated, and made conducive to the glory of God in the enlargement of Zion.

While these results have been accomplished through the instrumentality of the Board, the inquiry arises, How has all this expenditure of strength affected the two churches that originated this mission enterprise? Has the bestowment on others of their best gifts, weakened their own working force? Has the money which they have annually raised and liberally expended made them poorer? Far from it. At the organization of the Mission, in 1851, the two churches, as we have seen, had an aggregate membership of *five hundred and six.* At the present time, the membership of those two churches is *one thousand two hundred and eighty-seven;* and in the city, about *twenty-five hundred.* In 1851, their contributions for benevolent objects amounted, in the aggregate, to $2,117.36. In 1868 the sum reported was $20,766.84.

How forcibly do the above facts and figures illustrate these scriptures: "There is that withholdeth more than is meet, but it tendeth to poverty." "The liberal soul shall be made fat; and he that watereth shall be watered also himself." "Give, and it shall be given unto you, good measure, pressed down, and shaken together, and running over."

> "Give with no faltering hand,
> Give with no grudging heart;
> The cause is holy, — help it on, —
> You lend to the Christian's Lord."

The blessed results of this enterprise in the erection of churches, in establishing Sabbath-schools, in fostering the grace of Christian charity, in the conversion of souls, and in extending Baptist principles, should encourage the Baptists of Newark to go forward in their great and beneficent work. Much remains to be done. The city contains a population of over one hundred thousand. These six Baptist churches and three chapels, — what are they among so many? And the population is rapidly increasing. The advantageous location of the city, its broad and beautiful streets, its well regulated police, its commodious dwellings, its proximity to New York, and its railroad facilities, are attracting the attention of capitalists and manufacturers, and inviting families to make their homes where they may live better and cheaper than in New York. It is estimated that in twenty-five years there will be, within the limits of the city of Newark, two hundred and fifty thousand souls. Now it will not do to wait until these come. It is the part of prudence and piety to make ready for their coming. It would be no more than wise and provident to build one chapel every year. This would give the denomination the advantage of preoccupation. There need be no fear of these not being filled. It is astonishing how soon houses of worship gather congregations from the mass of those who are non-church-goers. When God calls ministers to preach the gospel, He will call the people to hear, and when Christians build houses for His worship, He will provide the means to fill them.

The duty, then, is imperative, to be on the watch for opportunities to extend the cords as well as to strengthen the stakes of our Zion. We are sacredly called upon to gird ourselves anew for the accumulating work we find at our very doors.

And we have every encouragment to be thus faithful. Our principles are gaining favor every year, and must continue to do so, as the community advances in intelligence and in freedom of thought. As men learn to think for themselves, to read the Bible for themselves, to repent of sins for themselves, to believe for themselves, and to obey Christ for themselves, they will seek the churches which have for ages "resisted even unto blood" the assumptions of civil and ecclesiastical tyranny, and which, discarding all the traditions of men, and fearlessly braving the sneers and misrepresentations of the world, have simply and earnestly required of all who may have sought admission into the kingdom of Christ, personal faith and obedience.

Surely, when we consider what has already been wrought by our denomination, we are compelled to acknowledge the hand of God, and to believe that He will continue to smile upon our efforts to advance His kingdom, and to maintain the honor of His word and the purity of His ordinances.

> " What though the gates of hell withstood,
> Yet must this building rise :
> 'Tis thine own work, almighty God,
> And wondrous in our eyes."

www.ingramcontent.com/pod-product-compliance
Lightning Source LLC
LaVergne TN
LVHW021411110826
845150LV00007B/1876

* 9 7 8 1 4 2 5 5 1 0 6 1 9 *